COUNTRY

Formal Name: Hashemite Kingdom of Jordan (Al Mamlakah al Urduniyah al Hashimiyah).

Short Form: Jordan (Al Urdun).

Term for Citizen(s): Jordanian(s).

Capital: Amman (with a population of about 2 million).

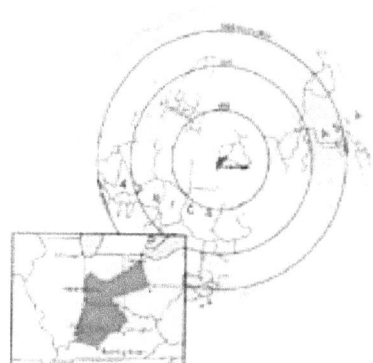

Click to Enlarge Image

Other Major Cities: Az Zarqa (472,830 inhabitants) and Irbid (272,681).

Independence: Jordan celebrates its independence on May 25, the day in 1946 on which Abdullah ibn Hussein al Hashimi was proclaimed King of Transjordan and a new constitution was enacted, replacing the British Mandate that ended three days before.

Public Holidays: Public holidays observed in Jordan include New Year's Day (January 1), King Abdullah's birthday (January 30), Labor Day (May 1), Independence Day (May 25), King Abdullah's accession to the throne (June 9), King Hussein Remembrance Day (November 14), and Christmas Day (December 25). In addition, religious holidays with movable dates dependent on the Islamic lunar calendar include Eid al Adha, the Feast of the Sacrifice; Eid al Fitr, the end of Ramadan; Muharram, the Islamic New Year; Mawlid al Nabi, celebration of the birth of Muhammad; and Leilat al-Meiraj, the Ascension of Muhammad.

Flag: The Jordanian flag consists of three equal horizontal bands of black (top), white, and green; a crimson isosceles triangle laid over the hoist side; and a small white seven-pointed Islamic star set in the middle of the triangle. The flag is an adaptation of the banner used in the Great Arab Revolt of 1916.

Click to Enlarge Image

HISTORICAL BACKGROUND

Jordan Region in Antiquity: From the earliest days of antiquity until the turn of the twentieth century, Jordan lacked a clearly defined political and territorial identity. Rather, its past was defined by the contending empires and kingdoms of which it often formed a part and by its geographic location as a buffer zone between the desert tribes to the east and the settled Mediterranean littoral to the west across the Jordan River.

Jordan in antiquity was characterized by small settlements on both sides of the Jordan River and after 2000 B.C. by a number of small tribal kingdoms based primarily on the East Bank. The

1

economies of these kingdoms relied chiefly on small-scale agriculture and metallurgy, but they also profited from the trade routes that crossed their lands, connecting Egypt and the Mediterranean with the Arabian Peninsula and the Persian Gulf.

In subsequent centuries, a succession of Israelites, Assyrians, Babylonians, Persians, and Greeks held sway over the Jordan region. Between the third and first century B.C., the Ptolemies and Seleucids competed for control of the area. In the process, both empires instituted an aggressive policy of Hellenization that brought prominence to such cities as Philadelphia (present-day Amman) and Gerasa (modern Jarash). The competition between the Seleucids and Ptolemies enabled the more southern Nabateans to flourish and extend their empire northward from their capital at Petra.

By the first century B.C., the Roman Empire and its vast legions had conquered the Seleucids, and by A.D. 106 the Nabatean kingdom, which had previously been a satellite of Rome, was formally annexed. After the division of the Roman Empire in 395, Jordan came under the control of the Byzantine Empire. Under Byzantine rule, Christianity became the official state religion of the region. Although it predominated in the cities and towns of the area, Christianity never gained a substantial foothold in the countryside, as it constantly competed with more traditional religious practices. Direct rule over the Jordan region and Syria was transferred in the sixth century to the Christian-Arab Ghassanid Dynasty, which was a vassal kingdom of the Byzantines.

The Coming of Islam: By 632 the eastern deserts of the Arabian Peninsula had been united under the leadership of the Prophet Muhammad and the banner of a new monotheistic faith— Islam. In 633, the year after the prophet's death, Arab armies entered the Jordan region, initiating a campaign of conquest and conversion in the name of Islam that would ultimately extend over the majority of the Middle East and beyond. Through the centuries, a changing array of Islamic empires held sway in the region—Umayyads, Abbasids, Fatimids, Seljuks, Ayyubids, and Mamluks. The defining characteristics of the Jordan region under most of these rulers was a remoteness from the seat of power; an Islamic population that was predominantly Sunni; a definitive decline in trade; a depopulation of the towns and other sedentary agricultural settlements, coupled with an influx of nomadic Arab bedouins; and an increasing reliance on the pilgrim caravan trade to Mecca.

The Mamluks were displaced in 1517 by the Ottoman Turks, who went on to dominate the region for the next 400 years. Jordan was included in the *vilayet* (administrative district) of Syria, but it continued to stagnate under the Ottomans and was mostly forgotten by the outside world until the nineteenth century. In the early years of the twentieth century, dissatisfaction with the rule of the Ottoman sultan brought to power a clique of reform-minded nationalist army officers known as the Young Turks. Despite their initial support of the Young Turks, the Ottoman Empire's many Arab subjects quickly turned against the new regime's secular-nationalist Turkification policies, as the local autonomy that they had hoped for failed to materialize. Combining an ability to merge the Arab nationalism of the region's urban intellectual class with the fierce independence of the desert tribes, the Hashemite (Hashimite) family of the Arabian Peninsula, who claimed descent from the Prophet Muhammad, rose to prominence as the spokesmen for the cause of Arab self-determination. The Hashemites were led by Hussein ibn

Ali Al Hashimi (1853–1931), the grand sharif and emir of Mecca and hereditary custodian of the Muslim holy places, and by his two sons, Abdullah (1882–1951) and Faisal (1885–1933).

The Arab Revolt and the Mandate Period: The outbreak of World War I provided the Arabs of the region an opportunity to rise up against their weakened Turkish rulers. With British support and aid, Sharif Hussein launched the Arab Revolt against the Ottoman Empire in June 1916. Britain during World War I eventually negotiated three differing and highly contradictory agreements concerning the future of the area—the Hussein-McMahon correspondence (July–October 1915) declaring British support for postwar Arab independence; the Sykes-Picot Agreement (February 1916) proposing the partition of the Middle East into separate British and French zones of control and influence; and the Balfour Declaration (November 1917), which stated British policy as viewing with favor the establishment of a Jewish national home in Palestine. Despite these conflicting policies, the Arab forces (militarily led by Faisal) and the British prosecuted the war successfully and in tandem.

The end of Ottoman domination of the region did not herald the much-anticipated rise of Arab self-determination. By April 1920 at the San Remo Conference, the decision came to enforce Allied rule of the Middle East via the mandate system of the League of Nations. While the French received Syria, the British obtained Iraq and Palestine; the latter was divided in two a year later. The eastern portion across the Jordan River was called Transjordan. An Arab administration headed by Abdullah (now an emir) operated this new entity on the East Bank under the supervision of the British commissioner for Palestine. A year later in September 1922, the British government and the League of Nations specifically excluded Jewish settlement from the Transjordan area of the Palestine Mandate in order to try to satisfy Arab aspirations and to fulfill Britain's responsibilities under the mandate.

Transjordan during this interwar period was sparsely populated with fewer than 400,000 inhabitants, mostly living in farming villages or nomadic desert tribes. Although British officials still tightly controlled most major policy decisions, Abdullah and his executive council did make certain strides toward the development of the country, especially with regard to infrastructure and education. Paramount among these developments was the creation of an indigenous military force led by British officers that was known as the Arab Legion. Abdullah was a faithful ally to Britain during World War II, and the Arab Legion served with distinction alongside British forces in Iraq, Syria, and Egypt. At the conclusion of the war, Transjordan achieved nearly full sovereignty from Britain. The country was proclaimed a kingdom and a new constitution instituted, although limited British base and transit rights persisted, as did the British subsidy for the Arab Legion.

Independence: Across the Jordan River in Palestine, violence and civil unrest between the Arab and Jewish populations had been escalating. Britain was overextended after World War II and unable to cope with the growing crisis. In fact, its eventual withdrawal from Palestine came on May 14, 1948. After the state of Israel was declared in the territory that had been designated the Jewish zone under a rejected United Nations-sponsored partition plan, armies from Transjordan, Egypt, Iraq, Syria, Lebanon, and Saudi Arabia advanced into the territory of the former Palestine. Because the Arab Legion was the most competent fighting force among the Arabs, Transjordan at the end of the conflict in early 1949 found itself in possession of much of the

West Bank of the Jordan River in addition to the eastern portion of Jerusalem, including the Old City and holy sites. Moreover, approximately 500,000 Palestinian Arabs took refuge in Transjordan or the West Bank.

With Abdullah now in control of both sides of the Jordan River, the official name of the country was changed in April 1949 to the Hashemite Kingdom of Jordan, a name found in the 1946 constitution but hitherto not commonly used. A year later, Jordan formally annexed the West Bank, a move that only Britain and Pakistan recognized. On July 20, 1951, a Palestinian radical assassinated King Abdullah as he entered the Al Aqsa Mosque in Jerusalem for Friday prayers. Abdullah's eldest son Talal succeeded to the throne, but because of a mental illness, he peacefully abdicated in favor of his son Hussein in August 1952. Hussein, who at the time was still a minor, would have to wait until May 1953 to formally become king.

King Hussein: For the four decades following his accession in the early 1950s, King Hussein and Jordan would have to navigate between two contradictory tendencies: the Hashemites' historical inclination toward conservatism, pragmatism, and close relations with the West on the one hand and the Middle East's frequent crises and the rise of pan-Arab nationalism on the other. By July 1957, the last British troops had left the country, although Jordan's relations with most of its neighbors (specifically Egypt, Syria, and Iraq) remained uneasy owing to the rise of socialist-leaning governments (aligned with the Soviet Union) that were ideologically at odds with Jordan's monarchic system of government.

In 1964, despite Jordan's opposition, the Arab League created the Palestine Liberation Organization (PLO) to be the sole representative of the Palestinian people. The creation of the PLO and its subsequent armed operations into Israel served as a direct challenge to Jordanian sovereignty and internal government control and brought about harsh Israeli reprisals. In June 1967, war broke out between Israel and its Arab neighbors. Despite a history of uncertain relations with Syria and Egypt, Jordan immediately entered the hostilities and paid a heavy price for its participation when Israel subsequently occupied all of its territory west of the Jordan River, including East Jerusalem. Additionally, another influx of approximately 150,000 to 200,000 Palestinian refugees crossed over into the East Bank.

In the years following the Six-Day War of 1967, Jordan was beset by internal turmoil resulting primarily from the tension between "native" East Bankers and the government of King Hussein on the one hand and the domestic Palestinian population led by various guerrilla organizations (of which the PLO was the most prominent) on the other. Low-level skirmishes between the two sides took place beginning in 1968, but it was not until September 1970 that full-scale fighting broke out. In what came to be known among Palestinians as "Black September," the Jordan Arab Army and the Palestine Liberation Army (PLA) bitterly fought into the month of October, causing severe material harm to the country and the deaths of an estimated 3,500 on all sides. The civil war culminated, after several broken agreements, in July of the following year with the routing and eventual expulsion of the Palestinian guerrilla fighters from the kingdom.

In 1973 Jordan did not directly participate in another round of Arab-Israeli fighting, although it did support Syria militarily during the war. In the ensuing years and into the 1980s, Jordan's regional position was characterized by fluctuating relations with nearly all of its neighbors, in addition to the unresolved Palestinian question, which King Hussein intended to resolve by establishing a confederated status between Jordan and a Palestinian state on the West Bank. This diplomatic approach was dispelled with the outbreak of the Palestinian intifada (uprising) against Israeli rule in the Occupied Territories in 1987. By 1988 King Hussein had officially revoked any Jordanian legal claim and administrative link to the West Bank, as Palestinian nationalist aspirations for an independent state could no longer be suppressed.

With the outbreak of the Gulf War in 1990, Jordan maintained an officially neutral stand and failed to condemn Iraq's annexation of Kuwait. Economically, the kingdom was hurt by the influx of refugees from the Gulf and by the embargo on its largest trading partner to the east. Diplomatically, Jordan was increasingly isolated as a result of its lack of support for Western military intervention (especially given its historically strong ties with the United States and Britain), which the majority of the Arab states supported.

Jordan's position improved dramatically in the mid- to late 1990s. In October 1994, Jordan signed a formal peace treaty with Israel, finally ending nearly 50 years of hostilities and finding agreement on issues such as borders, water allocation, security, and economic relations. Political parties were allowed to organize and to operate more freely than in the past, and despite boycotts by individual Islamist parties in certain instances, local and national elections were held more frequently. Additionally, a rapprochement with the United States, especially in military and economic matters, proved beneficial to the kingdom.

King Abdullah: After ruling Jordan for nearly its entire history, King Hussein fell ill and died of cancer on February 7, 1999. His eldest son Abdullah, who had been named crown prince just two weeks prior to Hussein's death, was sworn in the very same day. King Abdullah embarked quickly on a large-scale economic reform and political liberalization program, while simultaneously asserting his own personal rule and Jordan's historical role in regional diplomacy. Moreover, after the events of September 11, 2001, Jordan became a key ally in the United States-led "war on terrorism." It did not officially support the subsequent invasion of Iraq but did provide operational assistance during and after the invasion of March 2003. The removal of the regime of Saddam Hussein in Iraq brought unprecedented challenges and opportunities to Jordan. Economically, Jordan rose in regional importance as a secure staging area for various organizations and companies conducting business in Iraq. However, the instability and violence have sometimes spilled over into Jordan, as evidenced by a number of terrorist attacks by Iraqi-based terror groups inside of Jordan in late 2005.

GEOGRAPHY

Location: Jordan is located in the Middle East with Israel and the West Bank to the west, Syria to the north, Iraq to the northeast, and Saudi Arabia to the east and south.

Size: Jordan is slightly smaller than Indiana and encompasses a total land area of 92,300 square kilometers (91,971 square kilometers of land and 329 square kilometers of water).

Click to Enlarge Image

Land Boundaries: Jordan's land boundaries total 1,635 kilometers with Iraq (181 kilometers), Israel (238 kilometers), Saudi Arabia (744 kilometers), Syria (375 kilometers), and the West Bank (97 kilometers).

Disputed Territory: Jordan's last remaining territorial dispute was resolved in February 2005, when the interior ministers of Jordan and Syria signed an agreement ending more than 30 years of controversy over the exact demarcation of their mutual border through a land-swap arrangement in their border region.

Length of Coastline: Jordan has 26 kilometers of coastline along the Gulf of Aqaba.

Maritime Claims: Jordan claims a territorial sea of three nautical miles.

Topography: Jordan consists mainly of a plateau that varies in elevation from 700 to 1,000 meters and is divided into ridges by valleys and gorges and a few mountainous areas. The western edge of this plateau country forms an escarpment along the eastern side of the Jordan River–Dead Sea depression and its continuation south of the Dead Sea. The Jordan Rift Valley runs along the entire length of the border from the Yarmuk River in the north to the Gulf of Aqaba in the south; beyond Jordan, this great geological rift then continues through the Gulf of Aqaba and the Red Sea, gradually disappearing south of the lake country of East Africa. The maximum width of the Jordan Rift Valley is 22 kilometers. The valley floor varies in level, dropping from just above sea level in the north to 400 meters below sea level at the Dead Sea— the lowest point on earth.

From this depression in the western part of the East Bank, the desert rises gradually into the Jordanian Highlands—a steppe country of high, deeply cut limestone plateaus that average 900 meters in elevation and reach their highest peak at Jabal Ramm (1,754 meters). These highlands are an area of long-settled villages. Most of the East Bank is desert, part of the great Syrian (or North Arabian) Desert, and displays the landforms and other features associated with great aridity. There are broad expanses of sand and dunes, particularly in the south and southeast, together with salt flats. Occasional jumbles of sandstone hills or low mountains support only meager and stunted vegetation. These areas support little life and are the least populated regions of Jordan.

Principal Rivers: The Jordan River is the most important river in the country; it flows along and delineates the western border with Israel. Beginning in Syrian and Lebanese territory, the river flows south, first entering Israeli territory for 96 kilometers and then continuing in Jordan for its remaining 152 kilometers. The Jordan River's main tributary is the Yarmuk River; at the point where the rivers meet, the Yarmuk forms the boundary among Jordan on the south, Syria on the northeast, and Israel on the northwest. The Az Zarqa River, the Jordan River's second main tributary, is located entirely inside Jordan.

Climate: Jordan has a Mediterranean-style climate characterized by two contrasting seasons— the relatively mild and rainy months from November to April and the hot and dry summer during the rest of the year. During the summer months, temperatures average around 32° C with recorded highs of up to 49° C. In the winter, temperatures cool down markedly, averaging around 13° C. The dry desert and steppe regions of the country receive less than 120 millimeters of rain a year, but the precipitation increases with the rise in elevation in the highlands east of the Jordan Valley (from 300 millimeters to more than 500 millimeters, respectively, in the south and north). Indeed, frost and occasional snow can oftentimes be seen in Amman during the height of the winter season. In general, the farther inland from the Mediterranean Sea an area of the country lies, the greater the contrast between the two seasons and the less rainfall received.

Natural Resources: Jordan's main natural resources are phosphates and potash, which together constitute more than 40 percent of the mining sector and 14 percent of the country's domestic exports. Unlike many of its neighbors, Jordan lacks large oil and gas reserves and is highly dependent on imported energy sources. An energy diversification campaign has been hinted at; the country's numerous shale oil deposits (estimated at 40 billion tons) are the leading candidates for exploration and development.

Land Use: Water resources continue to be a major concern for the country. Only 3.3 percent of Jordan's land is arable, and only about 1.2 percent is planted to permanent crops according to 2005 figures. According to a 1998 estimate, Jordan had only 750 square kilometers of irrigated land (out of a total land area of nearly 92,000 square kilometers).

Environmental Factors: Jordan's main environmental issues include deforestation, overgrazing, soil erosion, desertification, and pollution caused by the misuse of agricultural chemicals, waste, and wastewater. In addition, with water demand outstripping secure and renewable supply sources, a severe shortage of water resources is of great concern to the country.

Time Zone: Greenwich Mean Time plus two hours.

SOCIETY

Population: Jordan's population was 5.1 million according to the 2004 census, up substantially from the 4.1 million recorded in the 1994 census. The population was estimated to have increased to 5.9 million by mid-2006 with an annual growth rate of approximately 2.5 percent. The country has a relatively low population density in comparison to the rest of the region— around 62 people per square kilometer. However, approximately 78 percent of inhabitants live in urban settings, and a large portion of the population (approximately 38 percent) resides in the capital, Amman. Much of the population consists of refugees of Palestinian descent stemming from either the 1948 Arab-Israeli War or the loss of the West Bank in 1967. Official United Nations figures put the number of registered Palestinian refugees living in Jordan in 2004 at 1.7 million, although independent and unofficial surveys estimated that residents of Palestinian descent exceeded 3.2 million, or approximately 60 percent of the total population. Foreigners, mostly from Egypt, Iraq, and Syria, reportedly constitute about 7 percent of the population. In the wake of the U.S. invasion of Iraq in 2003, anecdotal evidence has suggested a significant influx of Iraqis into Jordan, although concrete numbers are still difficult to obtain.

Demography: According to 2006 estimates by the U.S. government, around 33.8 percent of the country is less than 15 years of age, 62.4 percent is 15–64 years of age, and 3.9 percent is 65 and older. The median age of the population is estimated to be 23, and the sex ratio for the total population is 1.1 males per female. The birthrate is estimated at 21.25 births per 1,000. The fertility rate of women 15 to 49 years of age is approximately 2.63 children born per woman. The infant mortality rate is estimated at 16.76 deaths per 1,000 live births. The overall death rate is estimated to be 2.65 deaths per 1,000. The average life expectancy of Jordanians is around 78.4 years (75.9 years for males and 81.05 years for females).

Ethnic Groups and Languages: Approximately 98 percent of Jordanians are Arabs; the remaining 2 percent of the population is split among Circassian, Chechen, and Armenian minority groups. Arabic is the official and most used language. English is widely understood by the educated middle and upper classes.

Religion: The overwhelming majority of Jordanians (an estimated 92–95 percent of the population) are Sunni Muslims. Christians (including various denominations such as Greek Orthodox, Roman Catholic, Greek Catholic, Armenian Orthodox, Assyrian, Maronite, and assorted Protestant churches, among others) are the largest religious minority, constituting an estimated at 3–6 percent of the population. The rest of the population (approximately 2 percent) is made up of small communities of Shia Muslims and Druze, a religious group found extensively in the Levant whose beliefs combine elements of Shia Islam, Christianity, and paganism.

Education and Literacy: The Jordanian government estimates that the country's literacy rate in 2003 stood at 94.9 percent for men and 85.1 percent for women, for a total literacy rate of 90.1 percent. This statistic is impressive considering that the region averages a literacy rate slightly under 70 percent. In addition, primary and secondary education is free for every Jordanian and compulsory through the age of 15. The enrollment rate is reported to be 94 percent for primary school and 76 percent for secondary school. The country's educational infrastructure as of 2003 consisted of 5,376 primary and secondary schools (including public, private, and United Nations Relief and Works Agency schools) with 75,995 teachers and nearly 1.5 million students, as well as 21 universities (eight public, 13 private). Notably, females make up almost half (49.8 percent) of all university students.

The Jordanian government has been increasing spending on education over the past several years; 17.9 percent of the budget expenditure for fiscal year 2003 was allocated for education. Indeed, according to some estimates the government's investment in developing and expanding the public education sector alone stands at US$100 million dollars per year. Nevertheless, many middle- and upper-class families prefer to send their children to private schools. Measures have been taken in recent years to modernize and reform the textbooks and curricula used in public schools, with special emphasis on how Islamic culture is taught as well as on computer training and English-language instruction. These efforts are part of the Jordanian government's attempt to increase the global competitiveness of its future workforce.

Health: In comparison to most of its neighbors, Jordan has quite an advanced health care system, although services remain highly concentrated in Amman. Government figures have put total health spending in 2002 at some 7.5 percent of gross domestic product (GDP), while international health organizations place the figure even higher, at approximately 9.3 percent of

GDP. The country's health care system is divided between public and private institutions. In the public sector, the Ministry of Health operates 1,245 primary health-care centers and 27 hospitals, accounting for 37 percent of all hospital beds in the country; the military's Royal Medical Services runs 11 hospitals, providing 24 percent of all beds; and the Jordan University Hospital accounts for 3 percent of total beds in the country. The private sector provides 36 percent of all hospital beds, distributed among 56 hospitals.

According to 2003 estimates, the rate of prevalence of human immunodeficiency virus/acquired immune deficiency syndrome (HIV/AIDS) was less than 0.1 percent. According to a United Nations Development Programme report, Jordan has been considered malaria-free since 2001; cases of tuberculosis declined by half during the 1990s, but tuberculosis remains an issue and an area needing improvement. Jordan experienced a brief outbreak of bird flu in March 2006. Noncommunicable diseases such as cancer also are a major health issue in Jordan. Childhood immunization rates have increased steadily over the past 15 years; by 2002 immunizations and vaccines reached more than 95 percent of children under five.

Welfare: The welfare of Jordanian society is average when compared both regionally and internationally. According to the United Nations Human Development Report, in 2005 Jordan ranked ninetieth out of 177 countries, placing it solidly in the middle range, ahead of neighboring states such as Egypt and Syria but behind Saudi Arabia and Lebanon. The total government expenditure on social welfare for 2002 was slightly more than US$190 million; the vast majority of funding went to programs such as the National Aid Fund, the Social Productivity Program, and the Enhanced Productivity Program. Despite these efforts, approximately 30 percent of Jordanian society still lived below the poverty line in 2001. In early 2006, the government established the Social Solidarity Commission to oversee government efforts to assist the poor and to formulate new strategies for reducing poverty. Poor Jordanians currently receive direct assistance from a number of government agencies.

As part of its 2002 Plan for Socioeconomic Transformation (PSET), the government stressed public investment in health and education as a means of raising the standard of living. Goals included expanding and improving health care for the poor, including raising health insurance coverage from 75 percent to 100 percent of the population, upgrading primary health-care facilities, and enhancing the efficiency of hospital administration. The PSET has been superseded by the National Agenda for Reform. Initiated in 2005, this plan sets economic, political, educational, and social welfare goals up to the year 2015.

ECONOMY

Overview: Jordan is a small country with limited agricultural, water, and domestic energy resources—deficiencies that have hampered economic development and improvements in the standard of living. Over the past decade, however, the government has made an effort to highlight Jordan's positive economic attributes, such as its relatively well-educated and skilled labor force and its stability compared with many of its neighbors. Since the succession to the throne of King Abdullah in 1999, the government has attempted to undertake broad economic reforms with a strong emphasis on economic liberalization and privatization, thereby diminishing to some degree the state's previously heavy involvement in the economy and boosting the private sector.

This newfound commitment to macroeconomic stability and private investment-fueled economic growth is a departure from Jordan's past economic history. In large part because of increases in government spending and subsidies, as recently as 1989 Jordan suffered from double-digit inflation rates, a sharp devaluation of its currency, persistently high budget deficits, and large increases in its external debt. But from 1989 to 2004, the government closely adhered to International Monetary Fund–supported readjustment programs (six such programs), successfully achieving sustainable growth, controlling inflation, and reducing its deficit. These reforms, in tandem with improved international political standing, have allowed Jordan to enter into several important free-trade agreements with such markets as the United States and the European Union and to join the World Trade Organization.

The World Bank classifies Jordan as a "lower middle-income country." Despite the successes of the past decade, the economy is still vulnerable to relatively high levels of poverty and unemployment and to the endemic instability of the wider region. Services still overwhelmingly dominate the economy, and despite the recent growth of the manufacturing sector, looming competition from Asia could undermine recent advances. In 2005 the government initiated an ambitious National Agenda for Reform for the coming decade. On the economic front, the agenda commits the government to continuing the policies of recent years—job creation, increasing per capita gross domestic product (GDP) as well as overall GDP, and reducing the debt-to-GDP ratio.

Gross Domestic Product (GDP): Jordan's total GDP for 2005 was US$12.9 billion, up from US$11.5 billion in 2004 and US$10.2 billion in 2003. The estimated GDP growth rate was 3.2 percent in 2003, 6.0 percent in 2004, and 6.1 percent in 2005; growth of at least 5 percent is expected to continue in 2006 and 2007. According to figures for 2004, services (including finance, real estate, transport and communications, and government services) continued to dominate the economy, accounting for more than 70 percent of GDP. Industry contributed about 26 percent of GDP (including manufacturing, 16.2 percent of GDP; construction, 4.6 percent; and mining, 3.1 percent). Agriculture provided just 2.4 percent of GDP.

Government Budget: In 2004 the Jordanian government estimated government revenues (including grants) at US$4.15 billion and expenditures at US$4.37 billion, including capital expenditures of nearly US$1.1 billion. The budget deficit was equivalent to about 1.9 percent of gross domestic product (GDP). Despite projected revenue increases from robust economic growth, the deficit was expected to worsen to approximately 5 percent of GDP in 2005, primarily as a result of a reduction in foreign grants (a drop of about 50 percent) and an increase in government spending. Not including grants, independent sources estimated the budget deficit to be US$1.4 billion in 2005, or 11 percent of GDP, with a projected improvement to about 9 percent of GDP in 2006 and 7 percent in 2007 (but only 5.4 percent, 4.3 percent, and 4.0 percent, respectively, if foreign grants are considered). The government continues to struggle to curb expenditures (including reducing and eventually eliminating oil subsidies), but rising oil prices, high expenditures on defense and security (the largest single item), and limited potential for cuts in social spending have thwarted its efforts.

Inflation: Consumer price inflation in Jordan was reportedly 1.6 percent in 2003, 3.3 percent in 2004, and 3.5 percent in 2005; it was expected to rise to 3.9 percent in 2006. High oil prices and reductions in government fuel subsidies contribute significantly to inflationary pressures.

Agriculture, Forestry, and Fishing: Despite increases in production, the agriculture sector's share of the economy has declined steadily to just 2.4 percent of gross domestic product by 2004. About 4 percent of Jordan's labor force worked in the agricultural sector in 2002. The most profitable segment of Jordan's agriculture is fruit and vegetable production (including tomatoes, cucumbers, citrus fruit, and bananas) in the Jordan Valley. The rest of crop production, especially cereal production, remains volatile because of the lack of consistent rainfall. Fishing and forestry are negligible in terms of the overall domestic economy. The fishing industry is evenly divided between live capture and aquaculture; the live weight catch totaled just over 1,000 metric tons in 2002. The forestry industry is even smaller in economic terms; approximately 240,000 total cubic meters of roundwood were removed in 2002, the vast majority for fuelwood.

Mining and Minerals: Potash and phosphates are among the country's main economic exports. In 2003 approximately 2 million tons of potash salt production translated into US$192 million in export earnings, making it the second most lucrative exported good. Potash production totaled 1.9 million tons in 2004 and 1.8 million tons in 2005. In 2004 approximately 6.75 million tons of phosphate rock production generated US$135 million in export earnings, placing it fourth on Jordan's principal export list. With production totaling 6.4 million tons in 2005, Jordan was the world's third largest producer of raw phosphates. In addition to these two major minerals, smaller quantities of unrefined salt, copper ore, gypsum, manganese ore, and the mineral precursors to the production of ceramics (glass sand, clays, and feldspar) are also mined.

Industry and Manufacturing: The industrial sector, which includes mining, manufacturing, construction, and power, accounted for approximately 26 percent of gross domestic product in 2004 (including manufacturing, 16.2 percent; construction, 4.6 percent; and mining, 3.1 percent). More than 21 percent of the country's labor force was reported to be employed in this sector in 2002. The main industrial products are potash, phosphates, pharmaceuticals, cement, clothes, and fertilizers. The most promising segment of this sector is construction. In the past several years, demand has increased rapidly for housing and offices of foreign enterprises based in Jordan to better access the Iraqi market. The manufacturing sector has grown as well (to nearly 20 percent of GDP by 2005), in large part as a result of the United States–Jordan Free Trade Agreement (ratified in 2001 by the U.S. Senate); the agreement has led to the establishment of approximately 13 qualifying industrial zones (QIZs) throughout the country. The QIZs, which provide duty-free access to the U.S. market, produce mostly light industrial products, especially ready-made garments. By 2004 the QIZs accounted for nearly US$1.1 billion in exports according to the Jordanian government.

Energy: Unlike most of its neighbors, Jordan has no significant oil resources of its own and is heavily dependent on oil imports to fulfill its domestic energy needs. In 2002 proved oil reserves totaled only 445,000 barrels. Jordan produced only 40 barrels per day in 2004 but consumed an estimated 103,000 barrels per day. According to U.S. government figures, oil imports had reached about 100,000 barrels per day in 2004. The Iraq invasion of 2003 disrupted Jordan's primary oil supply route from its eastern neighbor, which under Saddam Hussein had provided the kingdom with highly discounted crude oil via overland truck routes. Since late 2003, an alternative supply route by tanker through the Al Aqabah port has been established; Saudi Arabia is now Jordan's primary source of imported oil; Kuwait and the United Arab Emirates (UAE) are secondary sources. Although not so heavily discounted as Iraqi crude oil, supplies from Saudi Arabia and the UAE are subsidized to some extent.

In the face of continued high oil costs, interest has increased in the possibility of exploiting Jordan's vast oil shale resources, which are estimated to total approximately 40 billion tons, 4 billion tons of which are believed to be recoverable. These resources could produce 28 billion barrels of oil, enabling production of about 100,000 barrels per day. A Canadian firm has conducted limited exploration in the area southwest of Amman.

Natural gas is increasingly being used to fulfill the country's domestic energy needs, especially with regard to electricity generation. Jordan was estimated to have only modest natural gas reserves (about 6 billion cubic meters in 2002), but new estimates suggest a much higher total. In 2003 the country produced and consumed an estimated 390 million cubic meters of natural gas. The primary source is located in the eastern portion of the country at the Risha gas field. The country imports the bulk of its natural gas via a recently completed pipeline network that stretches from the Al Arish terminal in Egypt underwater to Al Aqabah and then to northern Jordan, where it links to two major power stations. This Egypt–Jordan pipeline is estimated to supply Jordan with approximately 1 billion cubic meters of natural gas per year.

The state-owned National Electric Power Company (NEPCO) produces most of Jordan's electricity (94 percent). Since mid-2000, privatization efforts have been undertaken to increase independent power generation facilities; a Belgian firm was set to begin operations at a new power plant near Amman with an estimated capacity of 450 megawatts. Power plants at Az Zarqa (400 megawatts) and Al Aqabah (650 megawatts) are Jordan's other primary electricity providers. As a whole, the country consumed nearly 8 billion kilowatt-hours of electricity in 2003 while producing only 7.5 billion kilowatt-hours of electricity. Electricity production in 2004 rose to 8.7 billion kilowatt-hours, but production must continue to increase in order to meet demand, which the government estimates will continue to grow by about 5 percent per year. About 99 percent of the population is reported to have access to electricity.

Services: Services accounted for more than 70 percent of gross domestic product (GDP) in 2004. The sector employed nearly 75 percent of the labor force in 2002.

Banking and Finance: The banking and financial services sector is reasonably advanced, and foreign institutions are increasingly entering the Jordanian market. Jordan's Arab Bank, however, is still the dominant player in the sector, holding an estimated 60 percent of all assets. The Housing Bank for Trade and Finance is the second largest institution in the sector, followed by seven other commercial banks, five investment banks, two Islamic Banks, and eight foreign banks. Efforts by the Central Bank of Jordan to encourage mergers among the smaller domestic institutions have been hampered by the traditional family-oriented ownership of many of the banks, reinforced by the conservatism historically exhibited by the Jordanian banking sector. In addition to the domestic and foreign banks, several credit institutions provide specialized loans for housing, agriculture, industry, and rural and urban development.

Despite banking and finance scandals that plagued the market in the 1980s and most recently in 2002, the central bank is deemed capable of regulating the sector. In 2004 the government undertook a program to enhance supervision and update regulatory practices. Despite regional instability over the past six years, the Amman Stock Exchange (ASE), which was established in 1999, has confounded experts by exhibiting quite robust growth. In particular, the Iraq war in 2003 in effect led to a boom on the ASE that resulted in record levels of trading volume and share price increases.

Tourism: The tourism sector is widely regarded as underdeveloped, especially given the country's rich history, ancient ruins, Mediterranean climate, and diverse geography. Despite personal appeals by the king and an increasingly sophisticated marketing campaign, the industry is still adversely affected by the political instability of the region. More than 5 million visitors entered Jordan in 2004, generating US$1.3 billion in earnings. Earnings from tourism rose to US$1.4 billion in 2005. The fact that the bulk of Jordan's tourist trade emanates from elsewhere in the Middle East should contribute to the industry's growth potential in the years ahead, as Jordan is relatively stable, open, and safe in comparison to many of its neighbors.

Labor: The Jordanian labor force was estimated to total approximately 1.3 million workers in 2003, according to Jordanian government figures. A U.S. government estimate for 2005 indicated a labor force of nearly 1.5 million. An estimated 74.7 percent of the total labor force worked in the services sector, 21.5 percent in industry, and 3.9 percent in agriculture according to independent figures for 2002. The official unemployment rate was an estimated 14.4 percent in early 2006, but unofficial estimates were as high as 30 percent. Jordanians employed outside the country constitute a significant segment of the labor force; Jordanian government figures estimate a total of approximately 300,000 such workers abroad, mostly in the Gulf. Remittances from these workers are a significant source of income reflected in the country's balance of payments. Women constituted a growing but still small share of the labor force—about 13 percent of the labor force in 2004, more than double the level from a decade earlier. More than half of employed women worked in the education and health sectors.

Foreign Economic Relations: Jordan enjoys good economic relations with most of its neighbors and with much of the world. The kingdom was admitted to the World Trade Organization in 2000. In addition, it entered into a free-trade agreement with the United States that took effect in December 2001; an association accord with the European Union that took effect in 2002 and that is scheduled to turn into a formal free-trade agreement by 2014; and a new trade agreement with Israel in late 2004 that is supposed to lower trade barriers between the two countries. Jordan also has been an enthusiastic proponent of Arab free-trade initiatives both regionally and bilaterally; it entered into agreements with Kuwait and Saudi Arabia over the past five years and has been seeking similar arrangements with other neighbors such as Syria, Egypt, and Turkey.

Imports: Imports free on board totaled approximately US$7.3 billion in 2004 and US$9.3 billion in 2005 and were expected to increase to US$10.3 billion in 2006. The sharp rise in the value of imports was mainly the result of rising prices in global energy markets, a trend expected to continue in 2006. The main commodities imported include crude oil and petroleum products, machinery and transport equipment, food and live animals, textile fabrics, and manufactured goods. The primary sources of imports are the United States, China, Saudi Arabia, Germany, and the EU.

Exports: Exports free on board totaled approximately US$3.9 billion in 2004 and US$4.3 billion in 2005 and were expected to rise in 2006 to about US$4.8 billion The main commodities exported are phosphates, potash, fertilizers, agricultural products, clothing, and other manufactured products. The kingdom's main export markets are the United States, Iraq, India, and Saudi Arabia.

Trade Balance: Jordan had a negative trade balance of more than US$3 billion in 2004 and about US$5 billion in 2005, due in large part to the sharp rise in oil import costs. The deficit was expected to continue to worsen in 2006 and then to improve but still to exceed US$4 billion.

Balance of Payments: As a result of a substantial increase in its trade deficit (brought on primarily by rising world oil prices) and a slowdown in foreign aid and grants, Jordan's current account registered a deficit in 2005 of more than US$2 billion, and that figure is expected to worsen in 2006. By contrast, just two years earlier, the kingdom enjoyed a large current account surplus, and the current account was near balance in 2004. Jordan reportedly held more than US$5 billion in foreign reserves (excluding gold) in 2003, 2004, and 2005.

External Debt: Jordan's external debt totaled an estimated US$8.4 billion in 2004 and US$8.8 billion in 2005. The debt-service ratio was estimated to be 10.4 percent in 2004 and 9.2 percent in 2005. Jordan's main creditors were Japan, France, the United Kingdom, and the International Monetary Fund (IMF). Since the 1989 debt crisis, Jordan has benefit from debt rescheduling by the IMF and other multilateral lenders such as the London and Paris Clubs.

Foreign Investment: In recent years, regional political developments and domestic reforms and regulations have dictated the level of foreign investment in the Jordanian economy. Although official statistics on foreign direct investment (FDI) are not publicly available, according to United Nations figures there was a dramatic drop in FDI between 2000 and 2002 from US$787 million to US$56 million, in large part because of a deterioration in Israeli-Palestinian relations and fears of the potential economic dislocation caused by a war in Iraq. The level of investment reportedly was high in 2005–6 at US$1.1 billion, more than double the 2004 level.

Independent analysts have in recent years been encouraged by the government's increased commitment to liberalizing the domestic market and enhancing the investment climate for foreign capital. Measures have included an Investment Promotion Law, strengthened banking regulations and oversight, increased vigilance regarding intellectual property rights, and the lessening of restrictions on foreign ownership of domestic firms. In addition, after 2003 many foreign multinational corporations viewed Jordan as an important gateway to the new Iraqi market. Despite these advances, regulations persist barring foreign ownership in certain sectors such as customs, land transportation, and security, and investors have continued to complain about "hidden costs" arising from an unresponsive bureaucracy and conflicting jurisdictions.

Free-trade agreements with the United States in particular have brought increased investment in the manufacturing sector through the qualifying industrial zones. Moreover, privatization efforts initiated in 1996 have led to an expanded role for foreign firms in previously state-owned enterprises such as telecommunications and potash production. According to Jordanian government figures, foreign investment accounted for just over 41 percent of total investment on the Amman Stock Exchange in 2004.

Foreign Aid: Jordan is a heavy recipient of foreign aid and is dependent on these inflows to cover governmental budget deficits and provide industrial subsidies for its citizens. By one estimate, the kingdom has received nearly US$9 billion in aid (US$1.3 billion in loans, US$7.7 billion in grants) from the United States alone since 1952. As a result of political developments in the region over the past decade, U.S. assistance in the form of grants, loans, and military matériel has increased dramatically. Jordanian government figures put U.S. grants for 2005 at approximately US$700 million, a decline from the previous year's US$1.14 billion. In addition, since 2003 Jordan has been a recipient of heavily subsidized crude oil from Saudi Arabia and the United Arab Emirates. Official development assistance to Jordan was estimated to total US$500 million in 2004.

Currency and Exchange Rate: Jordan's currency is the Jordanian dinar (JOD or JD), which is equivalent to 1,000 fils and is pegged to the U.S. dollar at a rate of JOD0.709 per US$1.

Fiscal Year: Jordan's fiscal year coincides with the calendar year.

TRANSPORTATION AND TELECOMMUNICATIONS

Overview: Similar to its position in more ancient times, Jordan plays a pivotal role in the transportation needs of the surrounding region, primarily via road. Jordan is a significant conduit of goods and people to Saudi Arabia and other Persian Gulf states and continues to be a major transportation hub into and out of Iraq. Domestically, the country's road network underwent various improvements in the mid-1990s, helping to facilitate overland trade from such disparate markets as Turkey and North Africa. As in other aspects of Jordan's infrastructure and economy, reform and privatization have been the norms recently, especially in the telecommunications field.

Roads: Jordan is served by nearly 8,000 kilometers of paved roads. The country's main national artery is the 330-kilometer highway that links Amman to Al Aqabah. Over the past decade, the government has made efforts to improve the quality and capacity of the road network. By 2002 Jordan had more than 346,000 passenger cars, an additional 145,000 vans, and more than 14,000 buses. To further its efforts to become a pivotal transportation and economic center, in 2004 the government became the first regional state to institute a new road network sign system that would unify the region's highways in order to facilitate transborder commerce and tourism.

Railroads: In comparison to the country's road system, Jordan's rail network is underdeveloped and limited. The predominant passenger feature of the network is a section of the Hijaz Railway that runs through Amman, linking Syria's capital Damascus with the Saudi Arabian city of

Medina. Additionally, a twice-weekly express link between Amman and Damascus was established in 1999. Plans are currently in progress for expansions to the rail system, including upgrading the internal rail link between Amman and Az Zarqa and establishing an international link between Jordan and the Israeli city of Haifa. The vast majority of the country's 618 kilometers of track are devoted to transporting freight, predominantly phosphates, from outlying mines to Al Aqabah.

Ports: Jordan's sole port facility is located in the southern city of Al Aqabah on the Gulf of Aqaba. In 2002 Al Aqabah handled nearly 9 million metric tons of exported goods and approximately 5.2 million metric tons of imported goods. The port facility has the capability to handle bulk cargo vessels and tankers, in addition to having container and roll-on/roll-off facilities. Divided into three distinct port sections (the Main Port, the Container Port, and the Industrial Port), Al Aqabah has a combined 25 berths for various vessels and ships.

Although estimates vary, according to 2005 figures, the Jordanian merchant marine totaled 26 ships, 12 of which were foreign-owned. An additional facet of the Al Aqabah port is the regular ferry service that runs to the Egyptian port city of Nuweiba. This ferry service furnishes an important low-cost link between North Africa and the Persian Gulf region.

Civil Aviation and Airports: According to U.S. government estimates, by 2004 Jordan had 17 airports, 15 of which had paved runways and 13 of which had runways longer than 2,400 meters, as well as one heliport servicing the entire country. Jordan has three international airports— Queen Alia International just outside of Amman, Marka International in East Amman, and King Hussein International in Al Aqabah. Queen Alia International is the country's main air transportation hub and headquarters for the government-owned national carrier, Royal Jordanian Airlines, in addition to serving approximately 22 other international airlines. Marka International is used primarily for flights to other Middle Eastern countries and domestic flights to Al Aqabah. According to 2004 statistics, Royal Jordanian has a fleet of 16 Airbus aircraft of various types and offers scheduled services to destinations in the Middle East, North America, North Africa, East Asia, and the Indian subcontinent. Currently, Royal Jordanian is owned by the Jordanian government, which since 1994 has been looking to privatize the national carrier; further steps in that direction are expected in 2006.

Pipelines: In 2004 Jordan had approximately 743 kilometers of oil pipelines and 10 kilometers of gas pipelines, according to U.S. government figures. The country's energy infrastructure recently experienced a substantial expansion, as a 395-kilometer natural gas pipeline linking Al Aqabah with two major power plants in northern Jordan began operation in December 2005. This pipeline is the most recent extension of a pipeline network inaugurated in 2003 that originates in Egypt and supplies the Al Aqabah power station via a 265-kilometer underwater pipeline.

Telecommunications: Since the rise to power of King Abdullah in 1999, Jordan has undergone a serious and expansive reform effort in the telecommunications field. Building on the partial privatization efforts of the mid-1990s, whereby private companies were allowed to enter and compete in the telecommunications market, the state-owned Jordan Telecommunications Company was partially privatized in January 2000. As a result of these and other reform initiatives, such as an emphasis on infrastructure development and information technology training, Jordan in recent years has become a major regional center for telecommunications business and investment opportunities.

Figures vary as to the prevalence and usage of telecommunications equipment among the Jordanian population. According to Jordanian government figures, in 2004 more than 630,000 main telephone lines were in use, and Jordan had more than 1.6 million mobile cellular telephone subscribers. The number of mobile subscribers was expected to increase to 4.5 million by 2008. Relative to the rest of the Middle East, where cell phone use per 1,000 people was only 53 in 2001, Jordan is a regional leader in this aspect of telecommunications, averaging 167 per 1,000 people that year. In 2006 the Jordan's mobile phone penetration rate was estimated to be 41 percent. Additionally, Jordanians used an estimated 265,000 personal computers in 2003, up from 150,000 just three years earlier. Nearly 630,000 people were estimated to have used the Internet in Jordan in 2004 (up from 444,000 in 2003). Approximately 110,000 of these users subscribed, including 10,000 who had high-speed Internet access. Although high costs continue to limit ownership of personal computers, the population is able to access the Internet via the many Internet cafés and government-sponsored Internet centers that offer free access.

GOVERNMENT AND POLITICS

Political System: Since its inception, Jordan has been a constitutional monarchy; according to the constitution of 1952, the system of government is parliamentary with a hereditary monarchy. Structurally, the constitution divides the powers of the government into executive, legislative, and judicial branches. In reality, most power is vested in the king as the head of state, chief executive, and commander in chief of the armed forces. Through his discretion, the king appoints and may dismiss the prime minister; the president and members of the House of Notables (Senate), the upper house of the National Assembly; judges; and most other senior government officials. Moreover, the king has the power to suspend or dissolve parliament, suspend the holding of elections, declare war, sign treaties, and approve or promulgate laws. In summary, the monarchy (as an institution) and the king (as a leader) constitute the most important political foundations of the state; as a result, the average Jordanian citizen has very little ability to affect or change the government. The constitution does stipulate a long list of rights and duties conferred upon the citizenry and the personal freedoms that they enjoy. However, these rights and freedoms have been curtailed for indefinite periods of time in the past as a result of various internal and external crises. The constitution explicitly states that Jordan and its people are an integral part of the "Arab nation" and that Islam is the official religion of the state and Arabic the official language.

The king exercises executive authority through the appointment of his cabinet, or Council of Ministers, headed by the prime minister. The constitution requires every new cabinet to present its statement of policies and programs to the Chamber of Deputies, the lower house of the National Assembly; by a two-thirds vote of "no-confidence," this body can force the cabinet to resign. By early 2006, the cabinet had expanded to 24 ministers, responsible for an array of duties ranging from defense, health, and justice to social welfare and agriculture.

The National Assembly (Majlis al-Umma) has a bicameral structure: a lower house, the Chamber of Deputies (Majlis al-Nuwaab; also referred to as the House of Representatives), and an upper house, the House of Notables (Majlis al-Ayan; also known as the Senate). The lower house consists of 110 members who are popularly elected to four-year terms; six seats are reserved for a women's quota, an additional nine seats for Christians, and three more seats for the Circassian and Chechen minorities. The House of Notables is currently composed of 55 members appointed by the king to four-year terms. The constitution stipulates that the size of the upper house cannot be more than half the size of the lower house. Although vested with little actual power, in recent years the National Assembly has increasingly been active in publicly debating, amending, and approving legislation put forward by the king and government.

The judicial branch consists of a number of different courts with varying areas of jurisdiction. The system is made up of civil, criminal, commercial, security, and religious courts. Civil courts include, in ascending order of hierarchy, Magistrates' Courts, Courts of First Instance, Courts of Appeal, the Court of Cassation, and the Supreme Court. These courts handle the bulk of criminal cases, and each has jurisdiction over varying levels and degrees of criminal cases and types of appeals. The Higher Judiciary Council, which is appointed by the king and operates under the supervision of the Ministry of Justice, is responsible for appointing, promoting, and dismissing judges. Although officially independent, the judicial branch, headed by the Supreme Court, is subject to informal pressure and interference by the government and other family and tribal elements.

Administrative Divisions: The kingdom is divided into 12 governorates (*muhafazat*; sing., *muhafazah*): Ajlun, Al Aqabah, Al Balqa, Al Karak, Al Mafraq, Amman, At Tafilah, Az Zarqa, Irbid, Jarash, Ma'an, and Madaba.

Provincial and Local Government: Each of the kingdom's 12 governorates is headed by a governor appointed by the king. Central government control extends into local areas through these appointees, who are the sole authorities with regard to government ministries and projects in their respective areas. The governorates are broken down into smaller administrative divisions such as districts, subdistricts, municipalities, towns, and villages. In 2003 amendments to the Municipal Law were implemented, changing the electoral system for local governments. Under the revised law, half of all municipal and village councils that had previously been completely filled with directly elected members would now be appointed by the Ministry of Municipal Affairs as well as the head of the respective council.

In the interest of promoting decentralization, the government reportedly has formulated plans to redraw regional boundaries and to establish directly elected regional councils in addition to the existing municipal and other local councils. However, as of 2006 no such reorganization had occurred.

Judicial and Legal System: The Jordanian legal code has evolved from historical precedents based primarily on Islamic law (sharia), French law adopted under Ottoman rule, and British common law adopted more informally (through case law and statute) during the mandate period. Under the Court Establishment Law of 1951 and the constitution, the judiciary is officially an independent branch of government, although in practice the monarchy and executive branch exert heavy influence. Under the constitution and the law, Jordanian citizens are afforded due process; public defenders are available for defendants unable to obtain legal counsel, and defendants have the ability to challenge witnesses and the right to appeal.

The State Security Court, which consists of three judges (two military officers and one civilian), handles matters such as drug trafficking, sedition, and offenses against the monarchy. There have been concerns in the past over due process in the Security Court; some defendants claimed that confessions were coerced through torture, others were not given legal representation until just before the trial's beginning, and many defendants were held in lengthy pretrial detention.

Religious courts, based predominantly on Islamic law (sharia) when dealing with the majority Muslim population, have jurisdiction over personal status issues (marriage, divorce, child custody, and inheritance). Christian courts have jurisdiction over the Christian minority on similar matters, excluding inheritance cases. A major distinction between the legal processes of the religious courts in relation to the other courts is that in the majority of cases tried under Islamic law, the testimony of two women is equal to that of one man.

Electoral System: The Jordanian people exercise their democratic rights primarily through elections for the Chamber of Deputies. Two royal decrees issued by King Abdullah in 2001 and 2003, respectively, ushered in changes to the electoral system for the Chamber of Deputies. Among other changes, the reforms expanded the membership in this lower house of parliament, increased the number of constituencies, allocated constituencies based on geographic considerations rather than demographics, and lowered the voting age. Despite some controversy regarding these changes from opposition elements, members are elected to four-year terms through a secret popular vote on the basis of proportional representation. Suffrage is universal and open to all Jordanians 18 years of age.

Under the Jordanian political system, the king has the authority to convene and dissolve the National Assembly and to suspend the holding of elections. Elections were held for the first time in 22 years in November 1989, and there was a gradual liberalization of the political system throughout the 1990s. However, when King Abdullah succeeded to the throne in 1999, he suspended the elections that had been scheduled for 2001. This election cycle, the last to have been conducted in the kingdom, eventually took place in June 2003. The next elections are scheduled for 2007.

By law, the approximately 200,000 Jordanian citizens serving in the military, police, or other security services are not allowed to vote. Additionally, the royal family itself traditionally does not vote or take part in elections.

Politics and Political Parties: Political parties were officially banned in the kingdom until 1992, although in earlier elections the political affiliations of the candidates were known implicitly to the public despite the lack of formal political party affiliation. In 1992 this situation changed, as both houses of parliament adopted the National Charter that King Hussein had endorsed a year earlier. Among other issues, the National Charter formally allowed the establishment of political parties, subject to certain stipulations such as respect for the constitution and the idea of political pluralism.

Throughout the 1990s, numerous Jordanian political parties were created, dissolved, or subsequently merged. By the most recent elections held in June 2003, there were 31 recognized parties in the kingdom, four of which took part in the elections. In actual fact, there are three competing political blocs in Jordanian politics: Islamists (led primarily by the Islamic Action Front, the political arm of the Muslim Brotherhood organization and the main opposition party); various leftist, nationalist, and Baathist parties; and dozens of independent candidates mostly comprising tribal, conservative, or former government and business representatives closely allied with the monarchy. The end results were a solid victory for the pro-government and pro-monarchy bloc. The independents won approximately 80 seats; the Islamic Action Front ultimately took 18 seats (the party's lowest result in any election that it had contested since 1989); independent Islamists claimed five seats; and the Leftist Democratic Party, the sole representative of the leftist/nationalist bloc, gained two seats.

Mass Media: The constitution guarantees freedom of opinion and speech, in addition to freedom of the press and media, but all within the limits of the law. According to the U.S. Department of State, in practice there are significant restrictions in place curtailing the free operation of the media. Any criticism or defamation of the king or royal family is prohibited, as well as anything deemed to harm "the state's reputation and dignity." The government has used tactics such as the threat of fines, prosecution, and detention to intimidate journalists and encourage self-censorship. Moreover, informants and censors at printing presses oftentimes give the government advance warning if a particularly inflammatory article is slated for publication, thereby allowing the government to apply pressure on the publisher to change or remove the item. Additionally, the Press and Publications Law and the Press Association Law impose certain limitations on the accreditation of journalists and the operation of newspapers; more damaging perhaps is the government's unwillingness to advertise in newspapers not at least partially owned by the state. Jordanian radio and television are even more restricted in their freedoms than the press. Internet access in the kingdom is generally open and unrestricted, although there were past reports of government investigations into the sources of overly critical Internet sites and the temporary blocking of certain Internet sites deemed inappropriate by the authorities.

Despite these myriad restrictions, Jordan remains more open and tolerant of its domestic media than most of its neighbors. The judiciary, not the government, is the sole institution able to revoke licenses from domestic media organizations, and the government's ability to shut down press outlets is severely limited. Additionally, court proceedings are open to the media unless the court itself rules otherwise. The law ensures the freedom and independence of foreign media organizations operating in Jordan, and international satellite television and regional television broadcasts are not restricted.

Jordan had six AM, five FM, and one short-wave radio broadcast stations as of 1999, as well as a reported 20 television broadcast stations in 1995. A new radio and satellite station were scheduled to begin operations in June 2006 after two earlier delays. Jordanians had more than 1.6 million radio receivers in 1997 and 560,000 television receivers by 2000. Additionally, the country has six daily newspapers and 14 weeklies, as well as 270 other periodicals (with an average circulation of 148,000 in 1998).

Foreign Relations: Jordan's foreign relations have been characterized by a balancing act between competing interests and pressures. As a result of its geographic location, historical role, and large Palestinian population, the kingdom is an important player in the Middle East Peace Process. Since the signing of a peace treaty with Israel in 1994, Jordan's role in the Israeli-Palestinian conflict has been one of encouragement and moderation as it attempts to mediate between the two sides. Public and governmental sympathy with the plight of the Palestinians has periodically strained Jordan's relations with Israel, especially after the outbreak of the Second Intifada in 2001. More recently, tensions between the Jordanian government and the Hamas-led government of the Palestinian Authority have surfaced; in May 2006, Jordan arrested several Hamas operatives allegedly planning violent operations inside the kingdom. King Abdullah has consistently emphasized a negotiated settlement to the conflict based on past United Nations (UN) resolutions and previous agreements between the parties and has pushed for renewed talks on permanent status issues that would lead to a two-state solution. With the outbreak of hostilities between Israel and Hezbollah along the Israeli-Lebanese border in mid-July 2006, Jordan initially condemned the Hezbollah attacks. However, Israel's subsequent escalation of the conflict produced widespread outrage in the Arab world, including among Jordanians. In response, the Jordanian government called for an end to Israeli aggression against Lebanon and an immediate cease-fire.

The kingdom has traditionally followed a pro-Western foreign policy and cultivated especially close ties with the United States and the United Kingdom, although there have been glaring exceptions, such as Jordan's support for Iraq during the 1991 Gulf War. Jordan's diplomatic isolation after 1991 was gradually reversed as a result of its support for the Middle East Peace Process and its assistance in enforcing UN sanctions against Iraq throughout the 1990s. Relations with the United States have become especially strong, as U.S. economic and military aid to the kingdom has increased. Nevertheless, the Jordanian government must tread carefully in the face of strong domestic support for the Palestinian cause and opposition to U.S. Middle East policy and the Iraq war.

After the attacks of September 11, 2001, Jordan became a key U.S. ally in the "war on terrorism" and tentatively (although unofficially) supported coalition operations inside Iraq in 2003. The Jordanian government recognized and gave support to the Coalition Provisional Authority and subsequent Iraqi governments and agreed to train Iraqi police cadets in its facilities. However, King Abdullah, who has voiced support for the Sunni Muslim minority in Iraq, was the first regional leader to voice concerns about the possibility of growing Shiite domination in the Middle East, given the overwhelmingly Shiite composition of the Iraqi government. The biggest strain on Iraqi-Jordanian relations, however, is the terrorist threat. Terrorist groups based in Iraq conducted a number of attacks inside Jordan in 2005. For its part, the Iraqi government has alleged that Jordanian citizens are crossing the border to take part in the Iraqi insurgency.

Relations between Jordan and other Arab states have improved markedly in recent years. After Jordan began distancing itself from Iraq after the first Gulf War, a rapprochement with the Gulf States became possible. Additionally, after the death of King Hussein in 1999, King Abdullah began a movement to normalize relations with Lebanon and Syria. Shortly after his succession, Abdullah was the first Jordanian monarch to visit Lebanon in more than 40 years. Jordan was one of the first countries to provide the Lebanese government with humanitarian aid and diplomatic support following Israeli-Hezbollah hostilities along the Israeli-Lebanese border in July 2006. Relations with Syria also have improved, as evidenced by the increased movement of people and goods between the two states and the increase in high-level intergovernmental interactions in the past five years. Nevertheless, in 2006 Jordan expressed concern about alleged Syrian support for Hamas operations in Jordan.

With regard to Iran, Jordan remains concerned about the long-term regional implications of an Iranian nuclear capability. The king reportedly has voiced support for a nuclear-free Middle East and has pushed for a diplomatic resolution of the Iranian nuclear issue.

Membership in International Organizations: Jordan is a member of the Arab Bank for Economic Development in Africa, Arab Fund for Economic and Social Development, Arab Monetary Fund, Council of Arab Economic Unity, Food and Agriculture Organization of the United Nations, Group of 77, International Atomic Energy Agency, International Bank for Reconstruction and Development, International Chamber of Commerce, International Civil Aviation Organization, International Confederation of Free Trade Unions, International Criminal Court, International Criminal Police Organization—Interpol, International Development Association, International Federation of Red Cross and Red Crescent Societies, International Finance Corporation, International Fund for Agricultural Development, International Labour Organization, International Maritime Organization, International Monetary Fund, International Olympic Committee, International Organization for Migration, International Organization for Standardization, International Red Cross and Red Crescent Movement, International Telecommunication Union, Inter-Parliamentary Union, Islamic Development Bank, League of Arab States, Multilateral Investment Guarantee Agency, Non-Aligned Movement, Organisation for the Prohibition of Chemical Weapons, Organization for Security and Co-Operation in Europe (partner), Organization of the Islamic Conference, Permanent Court of Arbitration, Universal Postal Union, World Customs Organization, World Federation of Trade Unions, World Health Organization, World Intellectual Property Organization, World Meteorological Organization, World Tourism Organization, and World Trade Organization. Additionally, Jordan is a member of the United Nations (UN), and has played an especially active role in UN peacekeeping missions around the world in such places as the Congo, Georgia, Haiti, and Sierra Leone.

Major International Treaties: The most significant international treaty signed by Jordan is the bilateral Treaty of Peace with Israel of October 1994. Additionally, Jordan is also a party to many multilateral treaties, including international agreements on Nuclear Testing, the Non-Proliferation of Nuclear Weapons, Chemical Weapons, Biological and Toxin Weapons, Gas Warfare, Torture, Genocide, Human Rights, and Trafficking in Women and Children. Additionally, Jordan is a party to numerous international environmental agreements, such as those on Biodiversity, Climate Change, Climate Change–Kyoto Protocol, Desertification, Endangered Species, Hazardous Wastes, Law of the Sea, Marine Dumping, Ozone Layer Protection, and Wetlands.

NATIONAL SECURITY

Armed Forces Overview: The Jordanian Armed Forces (JAF) consists of the Royal Jordanian Land Forces (including the Special Operations Command), the Royal Jordanian Air Force, the Royal Jordanian Navy, and paramilitary forces (which normally fall under the control of the Ministry of Interior except during wartime or crises). By 2005 the armed forces totaled approximately 100,500 active personnel and an estimated 30,000 to 60,000 reserve personnel. The breakdown among the services was 85,000 in the army, 15,000 in the air force, and approximately 500 to 700 in the navy. The paramilitary forces totaled an estimated 10,000 personnel (consisting of the police force, border police, and desert patrol) under the Public Security Directorate of the Ministry of Interior, in addition to a reserve Civil Milita ("People's Army") with an estimated 35,000 personnel.

Foreign Military Relations: Since before independence, Jordan has had a tradition of maintaining a strong military relationship with the West, beginning with Britain and extending into the present with the United States. Throughout the Cold War era, U.S. military aid to Jordan was complicated as a result of their differing relations vis-à-vis Israel, so Jordan often had to seek assistance from other sources, including the Soviet Union and Saudi Arabia. After the peace agreement between Jordan and Israel in 1994, military aid from the United States (currently Jordan's main foreign backer) began flowing in earnest, with substantial quantitative and qualitative increases after the attacks of September 11, 2001, and Jordan's subsequent support for coalition operations inside Iraq after March 2003. Overall U.S. military assistance to Jordan was approximately US$207 million in 2005, down from a high of US$606 million in the aftermath of Operation Iraqi Freedom in 2003.

The kingdom has formal security agreements with the United States, Saudi Arabia, and Turkey and has conducted joint military maneuvers with Egypt, the Gulf Cooperation Council, France, Oman, Qatar, Turkey, the United Arab Emirates, the United Kingdom, and the United States. Additionally, Turkey allows Jordan the use of its airspace and facilities for training its pilots, and the United Kingdom provides Jordan additional military training as well.

For its part, the Jordanian Special Operations Command provides training to many of the region's Special Forces, such as those from Algeria, Kuwait, Lebanon, Libya, Morocco, Oman, Qatar, Saudi Arabia, and Yemen. Since the fall of Saddam Hussein's Baathist regime in Iraq, Jordan has provided the new Iraqi government with various arms transfers and military equipment to support the fledgling Iraqi security forces in addition to training Iraqi police recruits inside Jordan.

External Threats: With the conclusion of a peace accord with Israel in 1994 and the rapprochement with Syria over the past five years, the external threats that Jordan currently faces are in some respects at their lowest ebb since before independence. Moreover, the 2003 removal of Saddam Hussein and his regime has eliminated an erratic and potentially hostile neighboring threat. Nevertheless, the current climate in the Middle East does not lend itself to stability and has the potential to affect Jordan's security. The Iraqi government is still weak, and if the effort to build a viable state there fails, the ensuing security vacuum and anarchy could have a destabilizing spillover effect on Jordan. In 2006 Jordan reportedly was taking steps to strengthen security along its border with Iraq as a result of concerns about escalating violence and instability in Iraq.

The Israeli-Palestinian conflict remains a persistent threat to Jordan's wellbeing. Any outbreak of hostilities, such as the July 2006 conflict between Israel and Hezbollah, places Jordan in the delicate position of advocating strongly for Palestinian rights and a peaceful solution, while at the same time remaining closely aligned with the United States and peaceable toward Israel. Jordan is wary of the Hamas-led government of the Palestinian Authority following Jordan's May 2006 arrest of several Hamas operatives allegedly planning operations in Jordan. Economic and humanitarian difficulties in the Palestinian territories could involve Jordan with the problems of refugees and angry public sentiment, a development that could be destabilizing inside the kingdom. Additionally, the Iranian nuclear program has raised concerns throughout the Middle East and in the international community. Nuclear proliferation in the Middle East is a growing risk; Jordanian neighbors such as Egypt, Turkey, or even Saudi Arabia could in turn feel threatened by an Iranian nuclear capability and attempt to develop their own indigenous nuclear programs.

Defense Budget: The Jordanian government spent approximately US$950 million on defense in 2005, a slight increase over the preceding three years and totaling close to 9 percent of gross domestic product (GDP). Jordan's domestic defense industry is small and highly specialized, so arms imports and procurements from the West in general and the United States and Britain in particular are expected to continue.

Major Military Units: The Jordanian military is divided into the army, navy, and air force. The Special Operations Command (SOCOM) falls under the control of the army and is composed of two Special Forces brigades, one counterterrorist battalion, and one ranger battalion. Aside from SOCOM, the army (or ground forces) is organized into four geographic commands: Northern, Southern, Eastern, and Central. The Northern Command consists of one infantry brigade, one artillery brigade, one air defense brigade, and two mechanized brigades. The Southern Command consists of one armored brigade and one infantry brigade. The Eastern Command is made up of one air defense brigade, one artillery brigade, and two mechanized brigades. The Central Command is composed of one air defense brigade, one light infantry brigade, one mechanized brigade, and one artillery brigade. The reserve component of the ground forces is made up of one armored division that includes three armored brigades, one air defense brigade, and one artillery brigade. The navy is based at Al Aqabah and is equipped with approximately 20 patrol craft, three of which are specifically for inshore use. The air force is composed of two fighter squadrons, four fighter ground-attack and reconnaissance squadrons, three training squadrons, one transport squadron, two squadrons of attack helicopters, one transport helicopter squadron, and two air defense brigades. The air force is located at six air bases (ABs) throughout the country.

Major Military Equipment: According to figures provided by the International Institute for Strategic Studies, as of 2006 the army's fighting force is equipped with approximately 1,120 main battle tanks, primarily high-quality Al-Hussein/Challenger I main battle tanks (390 tanks) and older Khalid/FV4030 main battle tanks (274 tanks). In addition, the army has medium- and low-quality main battle tanks, such as the M60 Phoenix (approximately 280), Tariq Centurion

(90 in store), and the M–47/M–48 A5 (78 in store). The inventory also includes approximately 19 additional light tanks of the Scorpion model; more than 226 armored infantry fighting vehicles, mostly the Ratel–20 (an estimated 200) and BMP–2 (more than 26); approximately 1,350 armored personnel carriers, 1,200 of which are M–113A1/M–113A2 vehicles; an estimated 100 vehicles of the FV 103 Spartan model; and 50 additional BTR–94 vehicles. The army also is equipped with approximately 1,233 artillery pieces, ranging in size from 105-millimeter to 203-millimeter shells, as well as approximately 94 towed artillery pieces and 399 self-propelled artillery pieces; 740 mortars; precision-guided munitions (30 Javelin launchers, 310 M47 Dragon launchers, and 330 TOW missiles); and more than 4,800 rocket launchers. The air defense capabilities of the Jordanian army consist of more than 992 surface-to-air missiles, including 152 self-propelled (92 Gopher SA–13 and 60 Gecko SA–8 systems) and an additional 840 man-portable air defense systems of various models. The army's air defenses also consist of 395 antiaircraft guns, and some artillery/mortar locating radar capability.

Although estimates vary, according to the International Institute for Strategic Studies, the air force has approximately 100 combat-capable aircraft, 85 of which are fighters (16 F–16 Fighting Falcons, 54 F–5 Tigers, and 15 F–1 Mirages). The inventory includes 14 additional transport aircraft, mostly C–130 Hercules transport planes. Flight training functions are carried out by 13 CASA C–101 Aviojets and 15 Bulldog 103s. The air force has more than 40 attack helicopters (AH–1F Cobras) and 15 support helicopters (three S–70A Black Hawks and 12 AS–332M Super Pumas), in addition to approximately 56 older helicopters (the bulk of which are UH–1H Iroquois) that are used for utility purposes. Although there is some ambiguity as to the air defense capabilities of the Jordanian air force, it is known that the force possesses more than 1,120 surface-to-air missile systems (mostly I–Hawk MIM–23B, and some PAC–2).

The small Jordanian navy has seven patrol boats, three fast patrol craft for inshore use, and fewer than 10 coastal patrol craft less than 100 tons in size.

Military Service: The Jordanian military is an all-volunteer force; enlistment is possible from age 18. There is a reserve obligation until the age of 40. Personnel must serve 20 years to become eligible for retirement benefits.

Paramilitary Forces: Jordan's paramilitary forces number approximately 10,000 personnel, divided into the police force, border police, and desert patrol. The kingdom's paramilitary forces fall under the Public Security Directorate of the Ministry of Interior, except in times of war when they are subordinated to the Ministry of Defense. Additionally, a reserve Civil Militia ("People's Army") has an estimated 35,000 personnel (both men and women).

Foreign Military Forces: An estimated 1,000 U.S. military personnel were stationed in Jordan as of 2005, in addition to a smaller, undisclosed number of British military personnel in support of coalition operations across the border in Iraq.

Military Forces Abroad: Jordan is an active contributor to United Nations (UN) peacekeeping operations around the globe. Jordanian military personnel are serving in Burundi, Côte d'Ivoire, Ethiopia and Eritrea, Haiti, Liberia, Serbia and Montenegro, and Sierra Leone. In addition, there are Jordanian observers in Democratic Republic of Congo, Georgia, and Sudan. A small

Jordanian contingency force was deployed to Afghanistan in the aftermath of the campaign to remove the Taliban in late 2001. Despite having had an Armed Forces Law since 1964 banning the deployment of Jordanian forces overseas (subsequently amended in November 2001), by one estimate Jordan has contributed 22,000 troops in 16 countries on behalf of UN peacekeeping missions since 1989.

Police: The Jordan National Police (officially called the Public Security Force) is subordinate to the Public Security Directorate of the Ministry of Interior. Located in Amman, the national police headquarters has responsibility for police, security, and law enforcement activities for the entire country. The operations of the Public Security Force are divided into three major functions—administrative (routine crime prevention and the maintenance of public security); judicial (the conduct of criminal investigations and assistance to the public prosecutor's office); and support operations (training, logistics, public affairs, communication, etc.). Additionally, there are three major structural divisions for the police force—metropolitan, rural (small towns), and desert units. The Special Police Force (SPF) is a separate and elite branch of the Public Security Directorate that focuses primarily on combating terrorism. In addition, the General Intelligence Department (GID) reports directly to the king and is responsible for domestic and international security, espionage, and counterterrorist operations.

Internal Threats: Internal stability is an ongoing concern for the Jordanian government and the monarchy, and the regime relies on an extensive and efficient intelligence and security network to maintain order. Historical tensions between indigenous East Bankers and Palestinian refugees are still a potential source of conflict inside the kingdom, especially given that Jordanians of Palestinian descent make up the majority of the population. However, King Abdullah has made strides in projecting a more unified and inclusive Jordanian national image, and several of his top advisers are of Palestinian heritage, as is the queen.

The more worrying and potentially destabilizing threat is the rise in radical Islamist activities, including recent protests and terrorist operations on Jordanian soil. Since the September 11, 2001, attacks on the United States, Jordan has seen an increase in security trials aimed primarily at radical Islamists. The violent protests that erupted in the southern city of Ma'an in early 2002, ostensibly over economic issues and police maltreatment, were led by Islamist activists and took on a decidedly Islamist cast. In addition, radical Islamists perpetrated a number of serious terrorist acts inside Jordan in 2005. Anecdotal reporting from both the media and U.S. government sources has indicated that Jordanian nationals make up a segment of the foreign-born insurgency fighting in Iraq. Most prominent among these was Abu Musab al Zarqawi, who hailed from the town of Az Zarqa. He was killed inside Iraq in June 2006. There is a potential for these Islamist fighters to return to Jordan and become destabilizing influences inside the kingdom.

Terrorism: Terrorism is arguably the highest national security priority facing Jordan today. At least two separate security agencies, the General Intelligence Department and the Special Police Force, have been actively engaged in counterterrorist operations for decades. In past years, the threat was from nationalist Palestinian guerrilla movements, but today the threat emanates primarily from radical Islamist terror groups. In October 2002, a U.S. Agency for International Development official was shot to death in Amman. In 2005 groups affiliated with Abu Musab al

Zarqawi and his Al Qaeda in Iraq movement claimed responsibility for a number of attacks in Jordan. In August terrorists fired *katyusha* rockets at two U.S. Navy ships docked at the port in Al Aqabah; a Jordanian soldier was killed and a taxi driver in the neighboring Israeli town of Eilat was injured. In November Iraqi suicide bombers detonated themselves inside three Amman hotels, killing approximately 60 people and injuring many more. These attacks aroused in the public both opposition to the perpetrators and fear of the risks of too close a relationship with the United States.

Human Rights: According to the U.S. Department of State, the Jordanian government's human rights practices are still problematic, although respect in specific areas does exist. Whereas Jordanian citizens do exercise certain democratic rights and elect their representatives to parliament, they do not have any real ability to change their government; the king is the final and sole arbiter on the identity of the prime minister, the make-up of the cabinet and the upper house of parliament, and the general direction of government policy. Incidents of harassment directed at members of opposition parties have been reported in addition to certain restrictions on freedom of speech, the press, association, and movement. The most serious human rights problems stem from the operations of Jordan's security services. There are still widespread allegations of police abuse and arbitrary arrests, mistreatment, and in some cases torture of detainees, as well as denial of due process and lack of independence in the judicial process. Violence and discrimination against women are still common in Jordanian society, as are "honor" crimes. In addition, there is a continuing lack of full societal acceptance of Palestinians, as well as continued abuse of foreign domestic workers inside the kingdom.